Disappointingly Old

ROBERT ROGERS

To order additional copies of this book, contact:
Xlibris
844-714-8691
www.Xlibris.com
Orders@Xlibris.com

ISBN: Softcover   978-1-6641-0877-6
        EBook   978-1-6641-0878-3

Print information available on the last page

Rev. date: 09/28/2021

Published Documents

Book

Times Change
Boyhood and the Vietnam war

Poem Books

Thing I Know
Real life happenings

Love and Hate
Good and bad experiences

Love Poems
Men and women relationships

Love and War
Love and the meanings of war

Poetic Stories
Wanting and Lasting love

Robert welcomes your comments. Email him: rcrogersrobert772@gmail.com

Contents

Acknowledgements

For You

For Nina, For Nita

For Me

Disappointing Older Life

Living an older life is disappointing
I love that woman
Life changes
So have I
We crawl into that bed
She remains the same
I don't
The performance is gone
God! I do wish it would return
We kiss and touch
I close my eyes
Remember how it use to be
She seems content
I remain obedient
No choice
Only remember how it use to be
The sun rises
I cannot follow that synonym
Disappointment
Regret what was once mine
I cannot fill her desire
We simply hold hands
Kiss
Hard to forget
Old is disappointing

Don't Remember Things

I don't remember things
I search for where I put that coffee cup
Can't remember what I had for dinner Did I turn on the dishwasher?
I can describe the things I want, I just can't name them
Why can't I name that long curved yellow fruit?
Those beef meat strips
That sweet crunchy round thing that is picked from a tree
I keep a lot of lists
One in the kitchen to remind me what I need
One in the living room indicating what to do today
One I carry to the GYM for the settings on the treadmill
I remember the things I did when I was young
The problem is I'm getting old
I need to go for that dental appointment
I go there every three months
Where did I put that small round thing I call a key?
I forget how to get there
Turn on that GPS and let it guide me
If I travel a distance and the GPS fails, so do I What do I do?
I'm just getting old
It's disappointing
Staying home is my best choice
I just don't like it
I sit in the living room and read an interesting book
Mark the page and stand up
An hour later I cannot name the author Where did I store that vacuum cleaner?
I will search
I wish I could find a younger me

I Yearn

Because I'm getting older
Health issues are a problem
I hate getting those mammograms
I feel vulnerable
I just hope they find nothing
My only real concern is that my breasts are sagging
That under wire braw doesn't help I even struggle to get it fastened
I don't want to look old!
I can't read a book without those glasses I may soon need a little eye surgery
Getting in and out of that SUV is a problem
Cars are built for the young not the old
I can't shut the door or find the seat belt
I remember what a Fob use to be A chain hanging on a pocket watch.
Getting old is a pain

Getting to that bedroom takes some time
I slowly climb the stairs
The washing machine hates me
Dragging those wet clothes out is difficult
Stuffing them in the dryer isn't easy I need a maid
The creams and pills don't help much
I just do what the Doctor says
He may not understand what a woman wants
I want to feel and look a bit younger
I have my doubts
That young female nurse doesn't understand
She will later learn
I solemnly yearn

I'm Getting Old

God! I'm getting old
At least that's what I'm told
I wake at 5:00
Stumble through that bathroom door
Turn on the light and find those pills
I'm not sure it cures my ills
I do what I am told
I hope the Doctor is right
I don't feel old
It's just so
I can not do what I use to do
But I sometimes try
I slowly put on my shoes
Walk down the hall
Nude
Put my hands on the wall
Dawn those boxing gloves
Punch that hanging bag Sweat like hell
Is it useful? I can't tell
That sweat reminds me of a loving time
She was with me
We showered together
We were young
I remember that from time to time
I wish she were still mine
Time takes its toll
We all get old

Only God Knows

I walked in for that appointment The Doctor asked are you Pregnant?
I smiled and said I'm 70 Why would you ask?
Doctors specialize
Neurosurgery
ENT
Ophthalmology
May have forgotten female biology
Menopause ends at 40
A child could only be a gift from heaven
I wish I was 25 again
Carry that newborn in my arms
What a gracious charm
God knows
Life moves in a definitive gate
It's not a race
It begins at a 6-month pace
Enters the world with a crying smile
It emerges with an attached cord
Separates and begins an individual life
Enters the world with all its strife
Lives and grows
The cycle never ends
I goes' forever
The wonders of loving
God knows
We all get old

Personality Changed

I have changed
My personality no longer remains
The temper is short
I get angry
I don't know why
It's a different life
Age seems the blame
I'm not the same
I don't stand in line It wastes time
I'm in no hurry
It just makes me angry
I sit in the waiting room
Drink coffee
Its past that appointment time
I consider it a crime
I wanted to buy a race car
The salesman gladly helped
He sent me to the paper guy
I waited an hour and saw no-one
I loudly said I need help
The whole dealership could hear me
The salesman was frightened
I almost punched him
Help came soon
People make mistakes
Apologize
I criticize
Should have been right the first time
I'm angrily disappointed

Pervasive Technology

The new technology drives me crazy
That mobile phone is pervasive
It rules lives
And cause wrecks
Driving while searching a phone number is dangerous
I don't own an iPhone I'm too old to understand how it works
What happened to a telephone?
It slowly disappeared
My wife has a flip phone That's about as good as it gets
I can't even use it
Where are those numbers?
That mobile phone has great power
More than was needed to travel to the Moon
It will lead us to Mars soon
I'm too old to know
Credit cards are confusing
I have one only to buy online
I don't have a choice
Cash and checks are outdated
I often stand behind a buyer that purchases a candy bar
Pays with a credit card
Inserts the card and it is often declined
Must reinsert it a second time
He needs 52 cents
I tried to rent a trailer
Wanted to tow my antique car
With my 1984 Chevy
Cash and check not wanted
The car needs repairs but remains in my garage
That car and I are both old
I need to find my screwdriver and plyers
See if I can fix the thing Sometimes can't find my glasses
May turn the wrong screw
Find my grandson
Show him how to drive a stickshift

Poverty Unknown

Do I have enough money? Poverty may soon exist I'm older now and retired
I've worked all my life
I don't want to live with my daughter She has enough to care for
The neighborhood is getting richer
My rent is getting higher
I don't have the money to buy a house What shall I do?
Getting older offers a puzzle
It's tough to arrange the pieces
I just spread them in my mind
Hope I can put them together
Create a clear picture
When the money is gone all will be lost
And so will I
I may join the rest of the improvised
Live in a tent
Not my idea of a pleasant event
Gaining food and water can be a problem
So will companionship
Restrooms at McDonalds or City Hall
My daughter will care
Others may not
I struggle with my thoughts of poverty
Retiring and getting older can be painful
I tried to save more money
My plan failed
My life will change
It will come to an unknown end

Self Service

My favorite grocery store has self service
A bank of computers to scan the products
I have no idea how to use it
No sticker on the onions, peppers,
and celery What do I do?
I go the checker area and stand in line
The woman ahead has two carts filled with products
I don't have a reasonable choice
I reluctantly tolerate my decision
Credit cards are accepted to dispense gas for my car
I don' like credit cards
Don't know how to use it So what do I do?
I go into the gas station to pay with cash
I wait behind the guy buying a coke
Naturally, he pays with a credit card
Talks at length with the young
woman behind the counter

Get your coke and let me pay!
Went to Home Depot to buy a gallon of paint
Can't scan without approval
Paint when consumed is dangerous
Must prove I'm an adult
Only one isolated area to pay with cash
But they do accept my Military discount
Tried to buy some whisky at the liquor store
Cash not accepted
They don't want to get robbed
Might be a reasonable choice
We were once, more civilized
When I go into town, I strap on my 9mm
I know how to use it I'm not sure others do
We're moving to a card holding wild country
I do myself a self-protective service
As I get older, I tolerate this different world
But I'm disappointed and frustratingly sad

Sexual Disappointment

As an older woman
I'm disappointed
I don't seem to enjoy sex like I once did The motivation is dwindling
I probably should stop drinking that wine
I want to be intimate, but I don't respond well
I don't think its his fault
It's mine
They call it Sexual Disfunction
I thought only men had that problem
I was wrong
I'm told to exercise and lose some weight
OK, I doubt that will solve the problem
Disappointment may linger
The man is capable and willing
I just seem to let him down In two ways
I'm going to watch my diet Buy a treadmill Stop drinking
that wine Is there a Viagra for women?
Perhaps just an aging problem
A motivational disappointment
I need some way to get more excited
That alone may solve my problem
Perhaps I'm just getting too old
Sexual contact seems to cause a bit of pain
I want to sexually remain Troubling
I don't share my problem
They just would not understand
Disappointment is a moderate word

Vulnerably Old

As we get older We are more vulnerable The phone calls seem real:
1. "Your two-hundred-dollar purchase from Amazon cannot
be fulfilled press 1 to talk to a representative"
2. "Your purchase order 2567390 is being held please press 2 to solve this problem"
3. "Your Microsoft account will expire in 24 hours just provide us
your checking account information to solve this problem"
4. "We have detected that an agency has stollen your Social
Security number press 2 to help resolve the problem"
5. "Your VISA card has a 528 dollar unauthorized purchase
press 1 to talk to our credit card representative"
6. "Your grandson needs emergency money we can
help press 1 to receive more information"
The list is pervasive
The calls seem real
The scammers target the aging population
Why? Because they are acceptable
Believe what people say
Reluctant to dismiss the calls They might be true What can we do?
Press "Delete!"
No reputable company or agency will telephone to solve a compelling problem
The aging often experience abuse
Physical
Financial
Neglect
Sexual
They don't report abuse to friends, family, or authorities
Vulnerability is more than disappointing.
Abuse is criminal

You're Old

You're "old"
That's what the doctor said
You are 80
And have a long-standing heart problem
It comes with age, gender, and genetics A heart
attack is not like the movies You won't clutch
your chest in panic Fall backward to the floor
We all are different and the same
Nothing lasts forever
Growing older continues
A stent can be surgically inserted
Increase blood flow to the heart
The effects of surgery can be unpredictable
There are a lot of medications that can help
Lower cholesterol

Prevent blood clots
Reduce blood pressure
Treat heart failure
You can still live a full life
Age has its tole
We hurt
Walk slow Don't see well
Bump into doors and chairs
Laugh at what aging brings
When we get old miracles can happen
Bones can be replaced
It's amazing that a hip, knee, ankle can be repaired
All a common occurrence when growing old
Aging never stops
It's disappointing

Printed in the United States
by Baker & Taylor Publisher Services